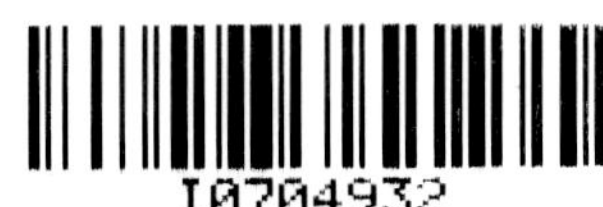

Name: ....

Address: ....

JESUS COLORING BOOKS

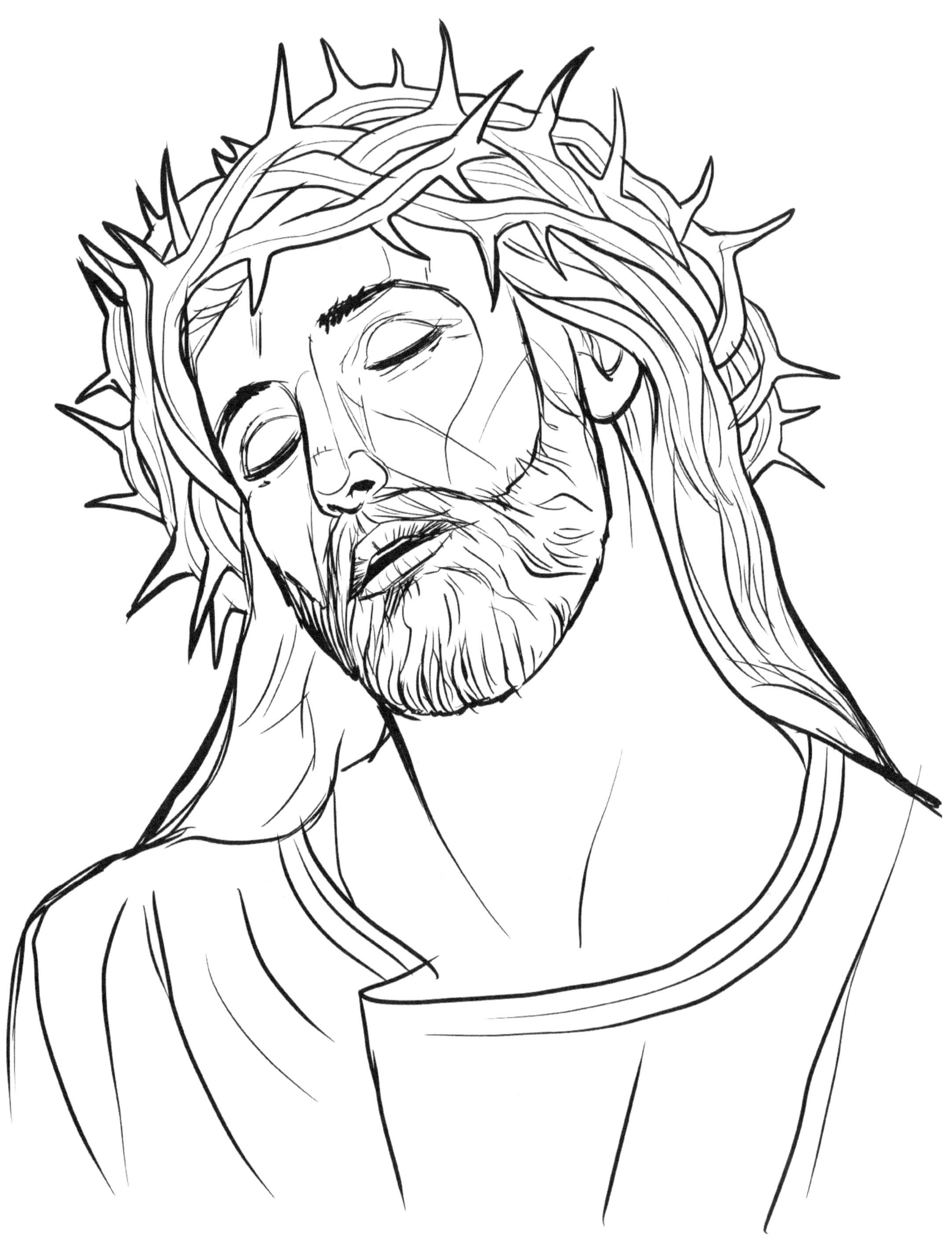

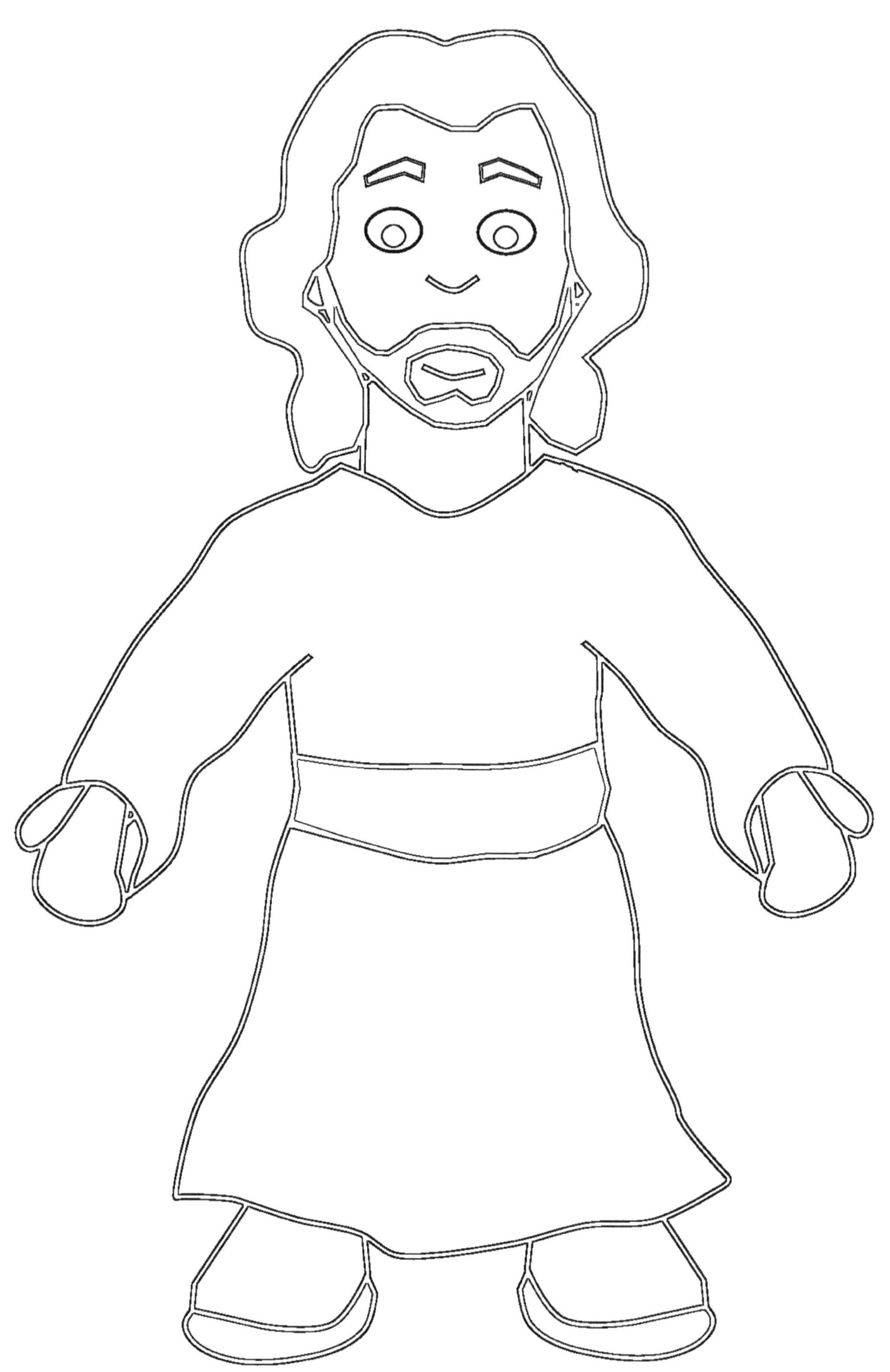

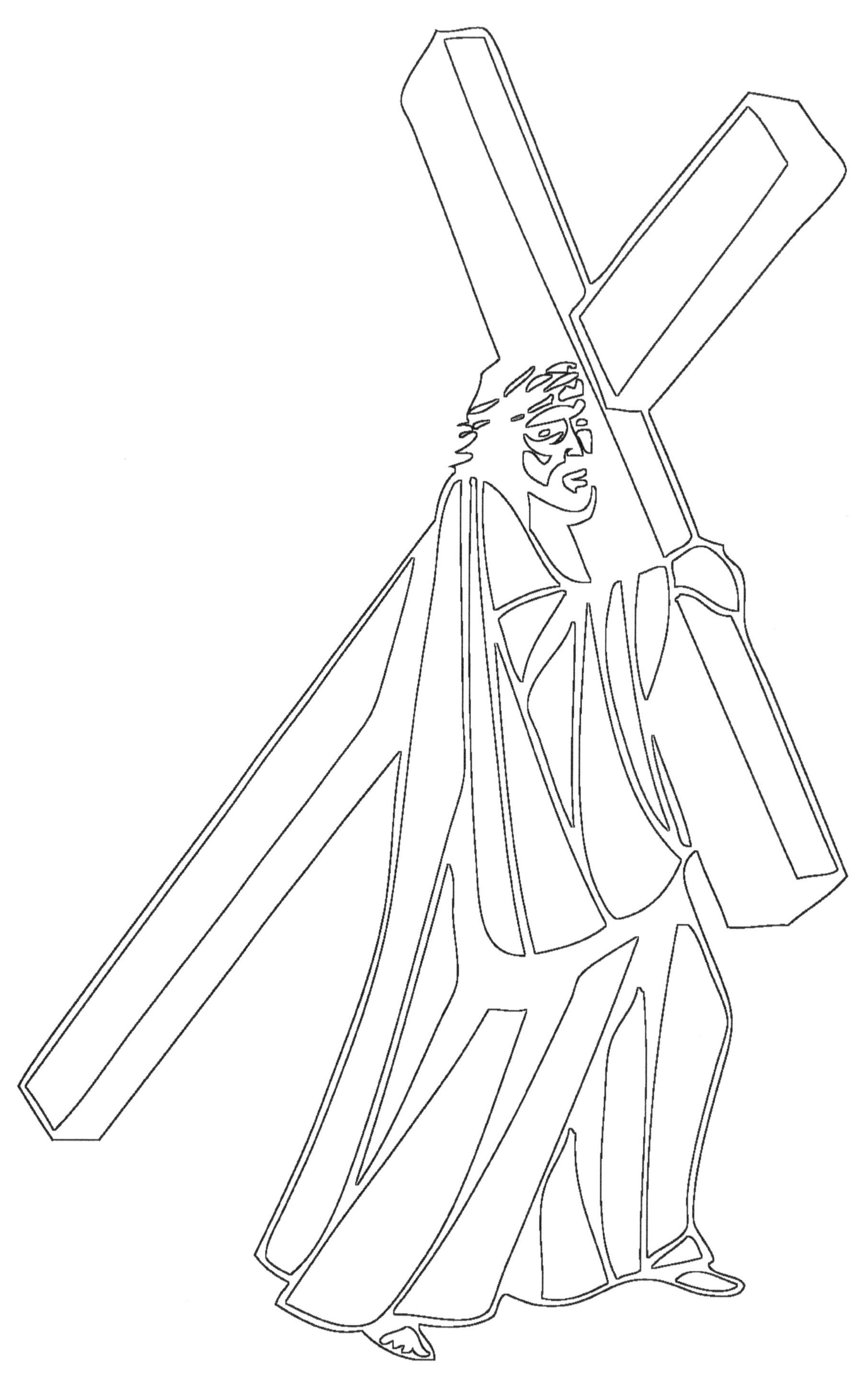

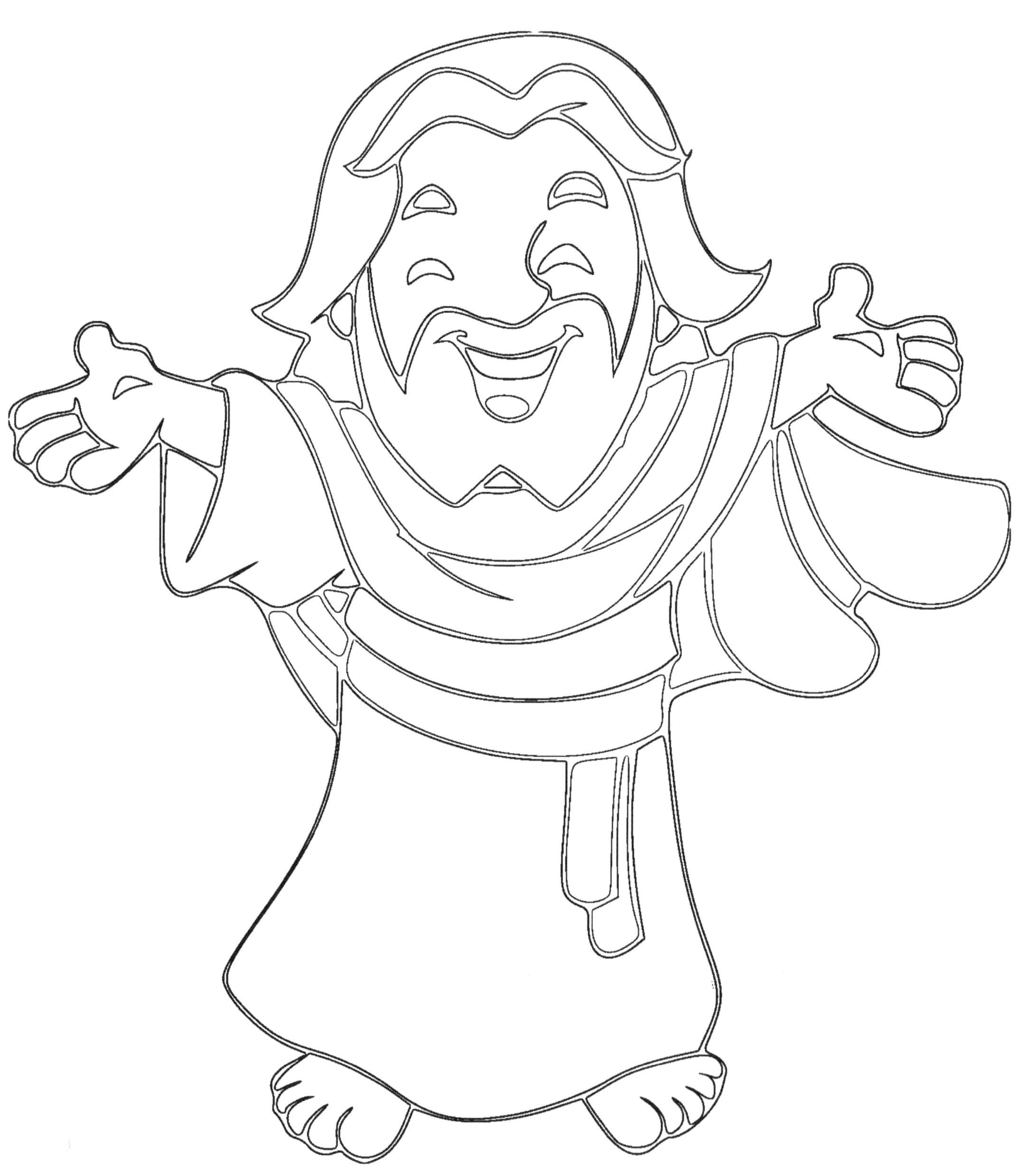

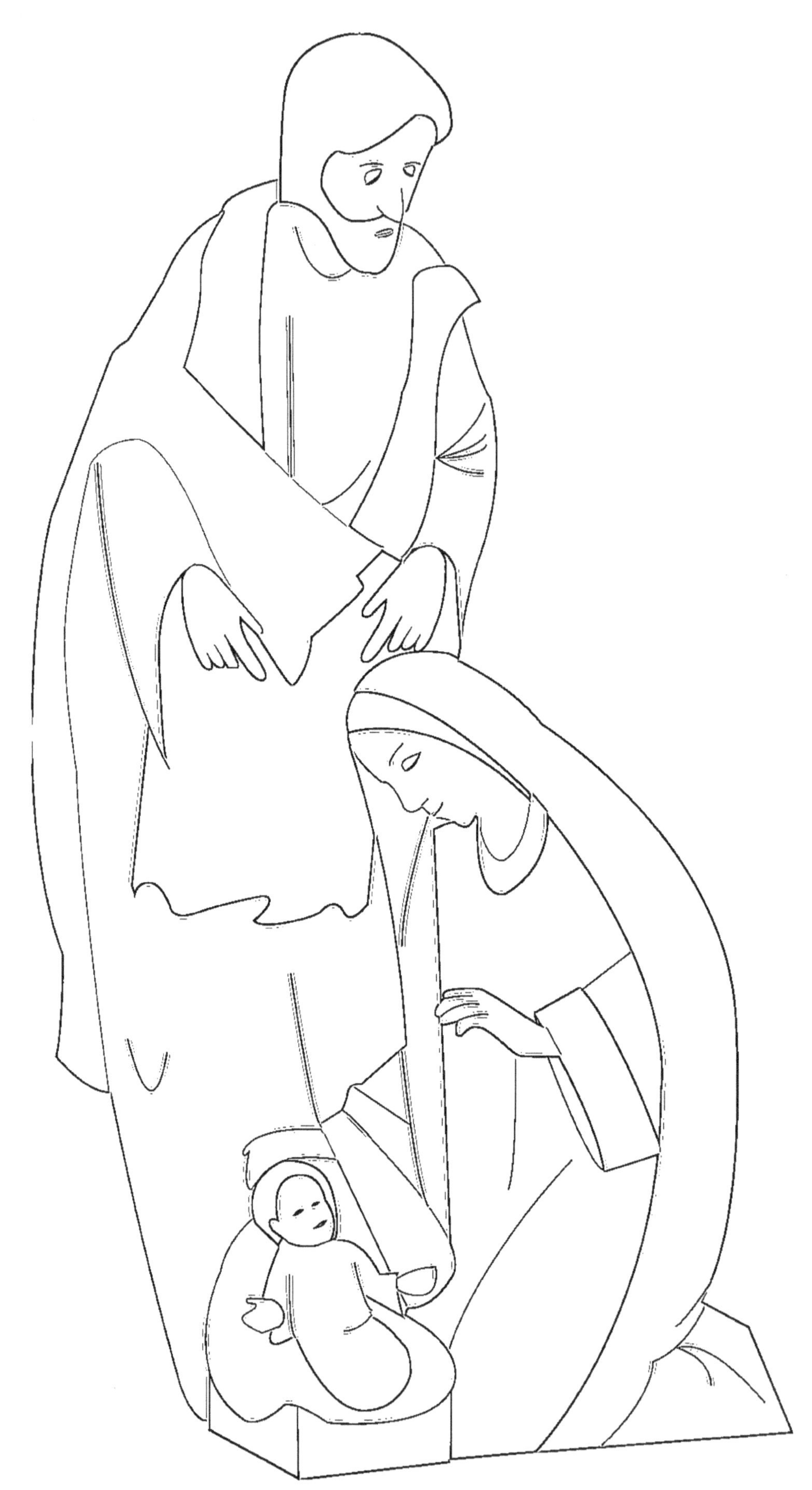

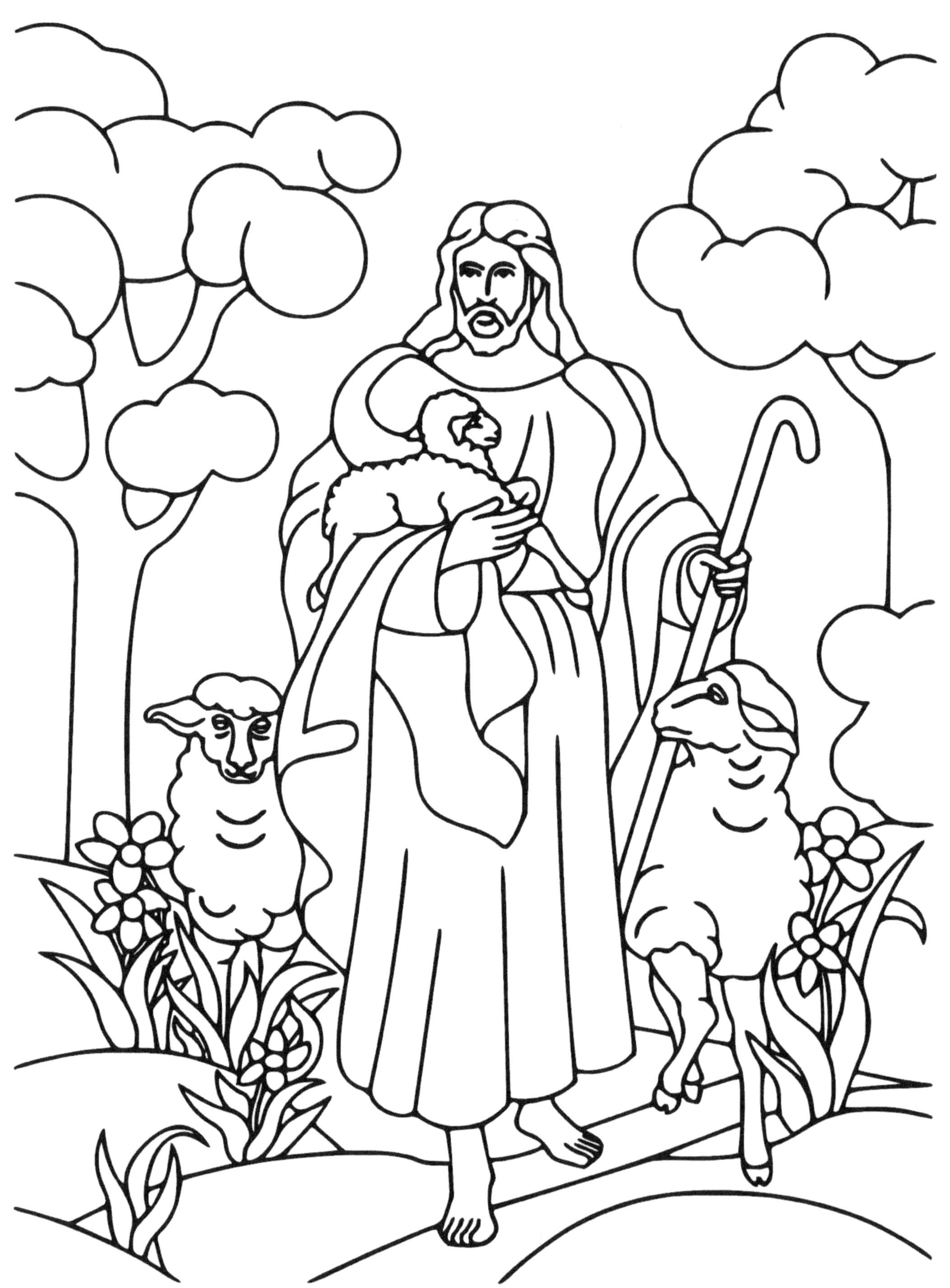

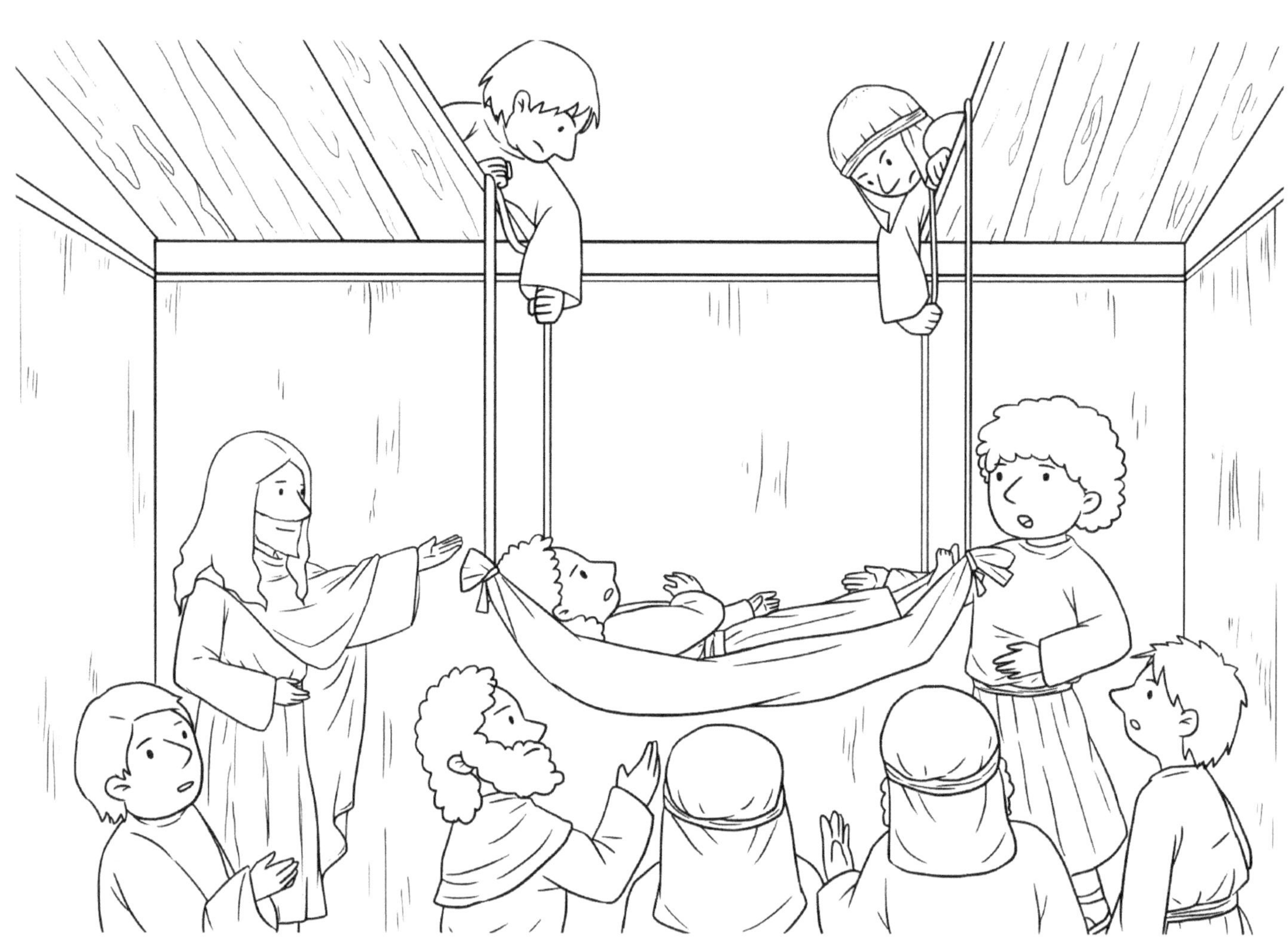

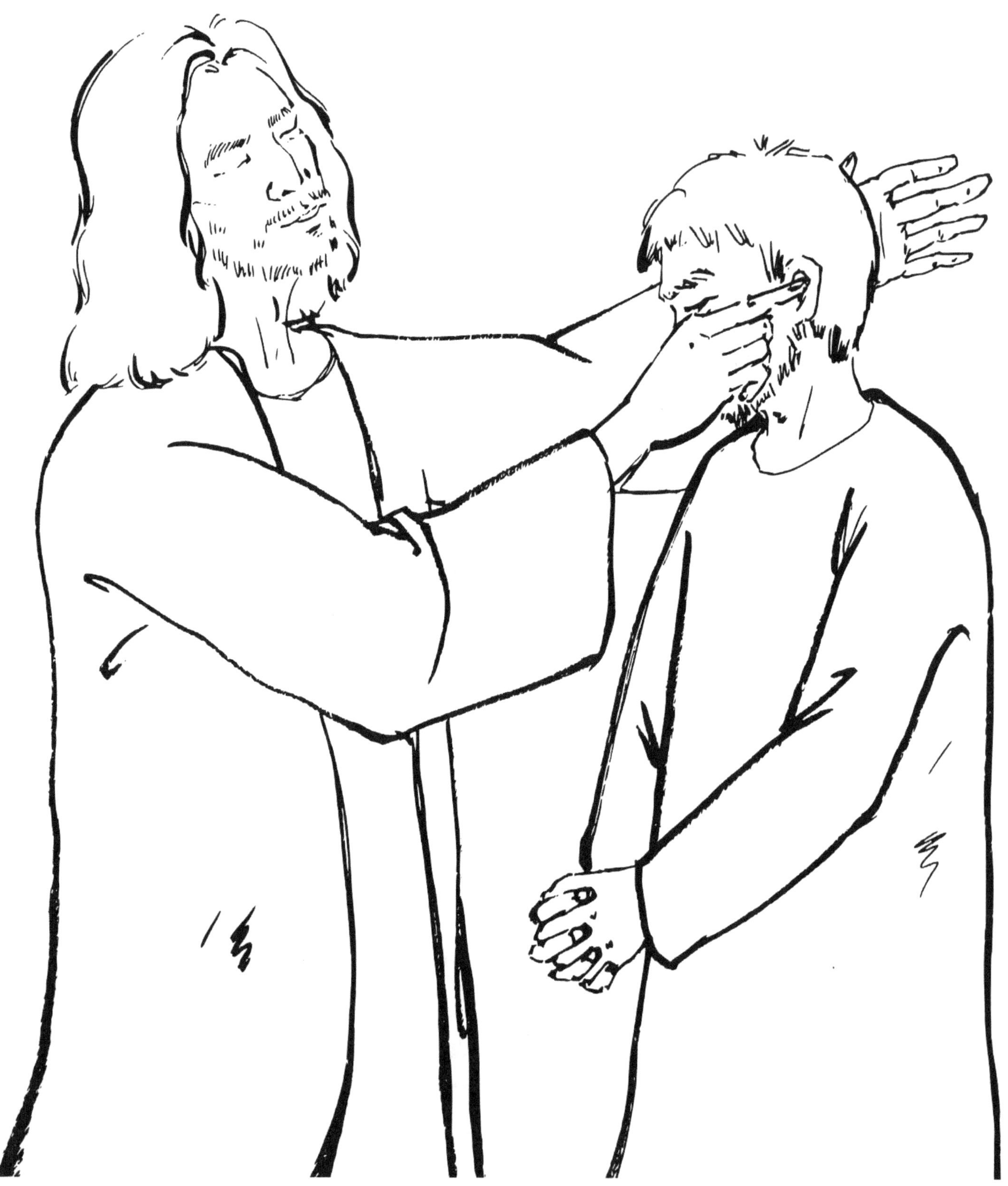

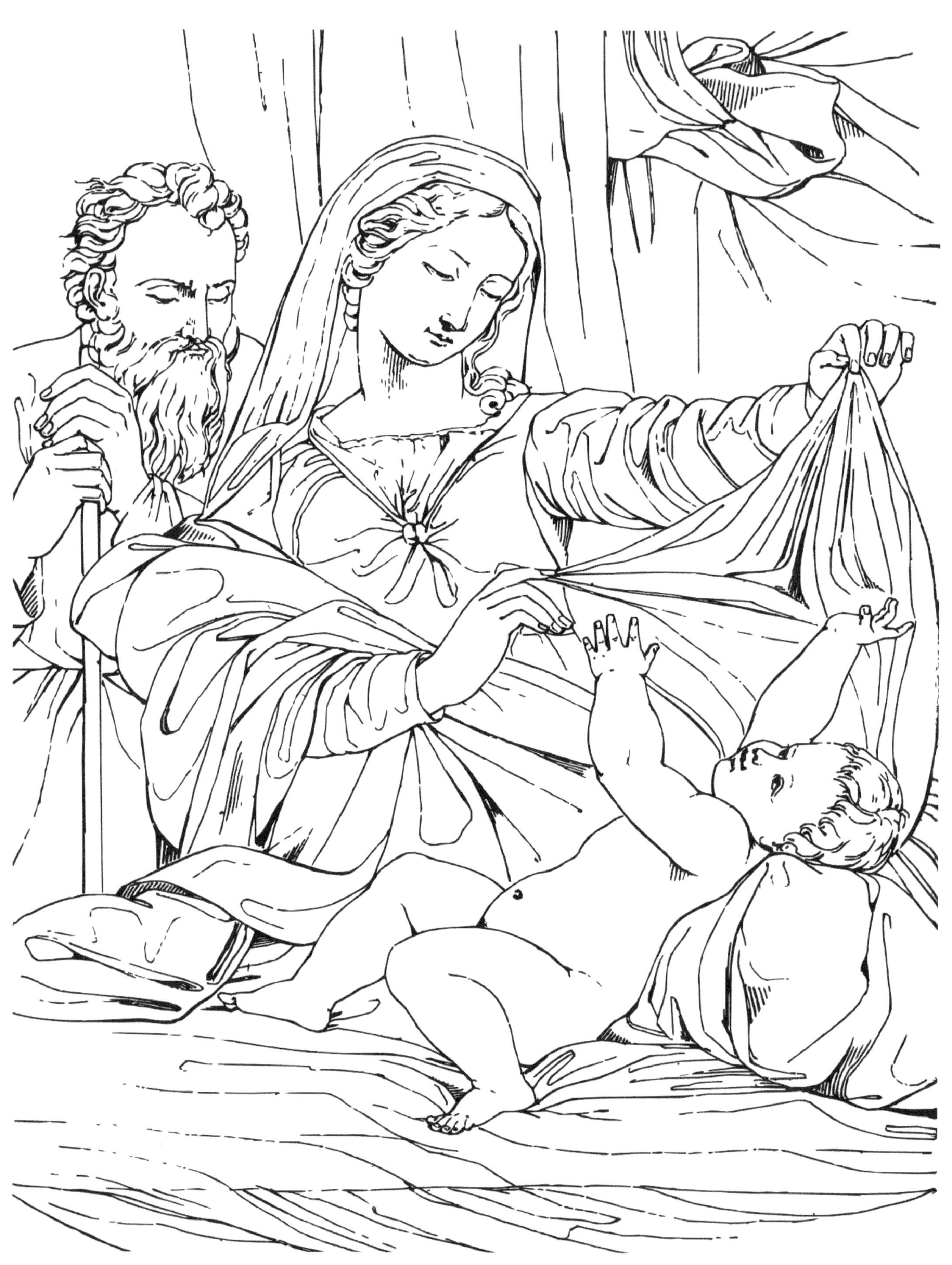

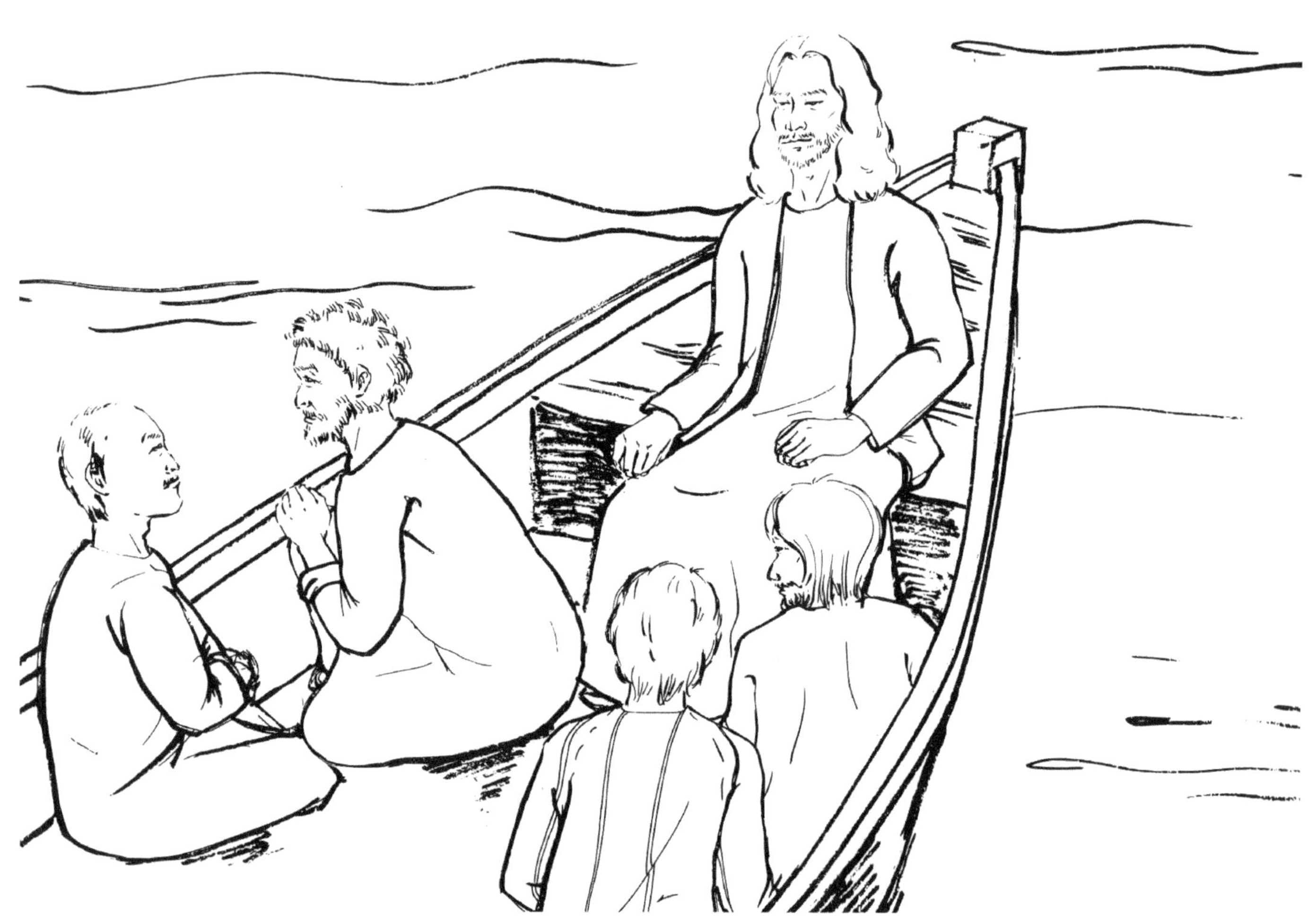

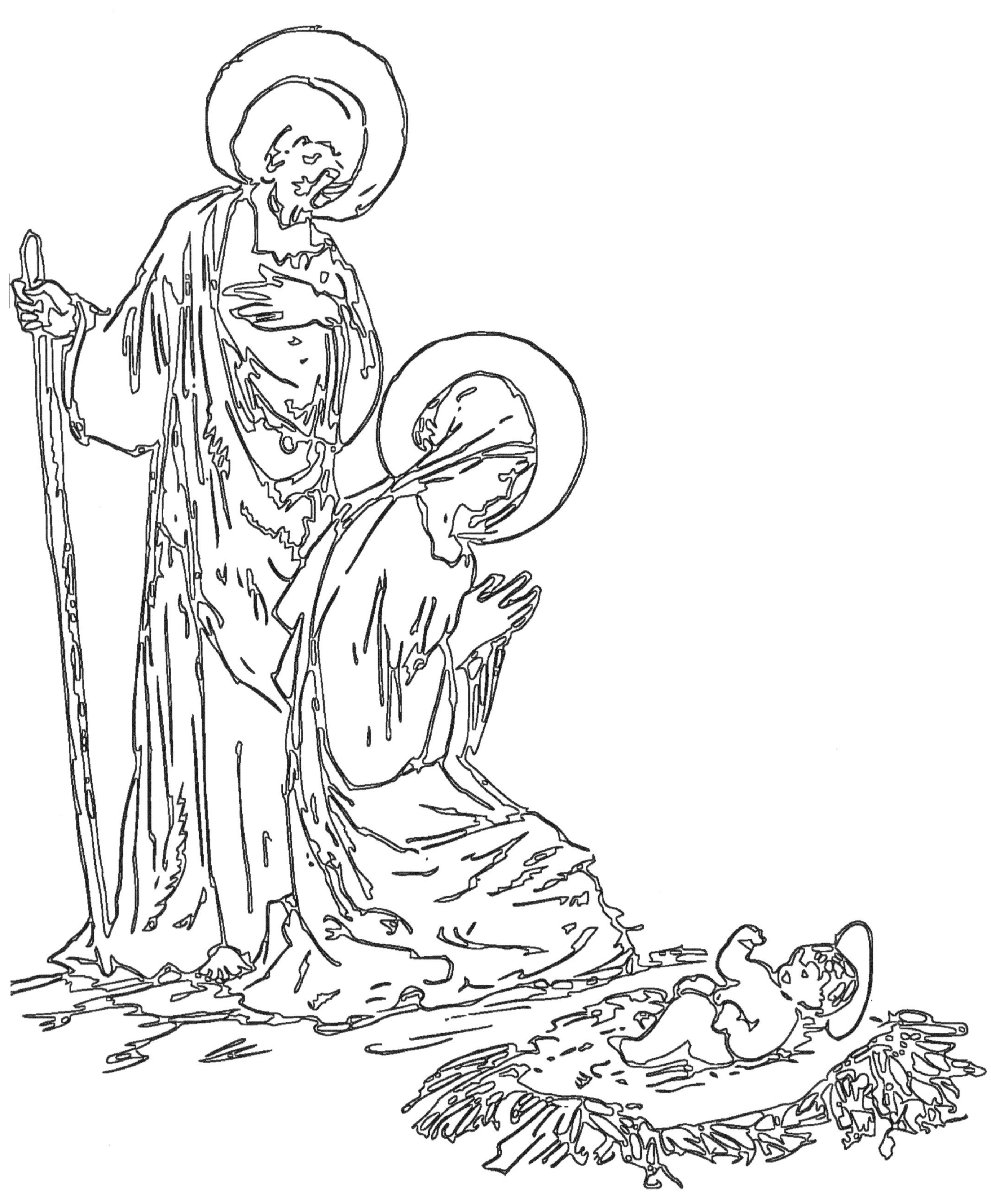

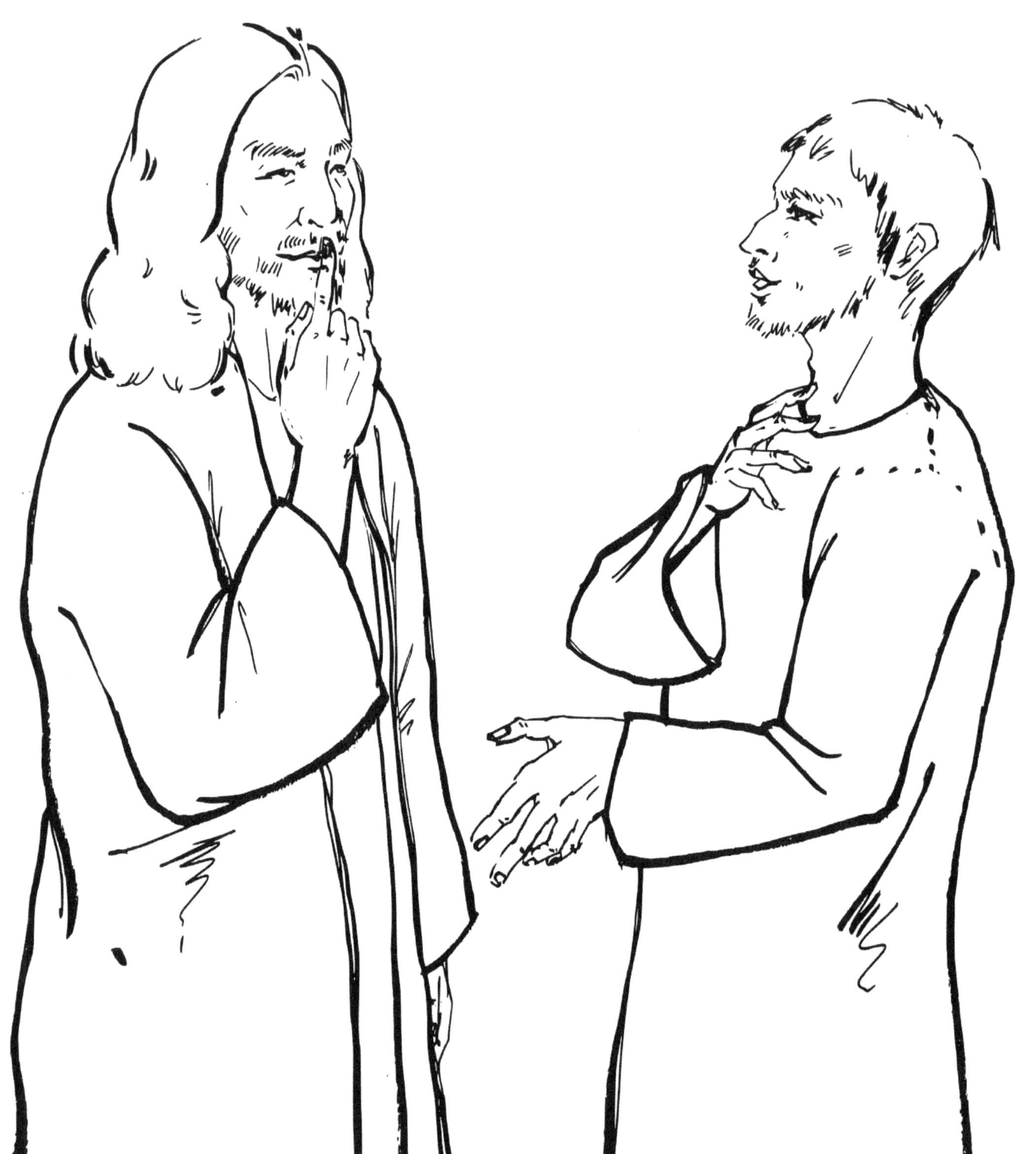

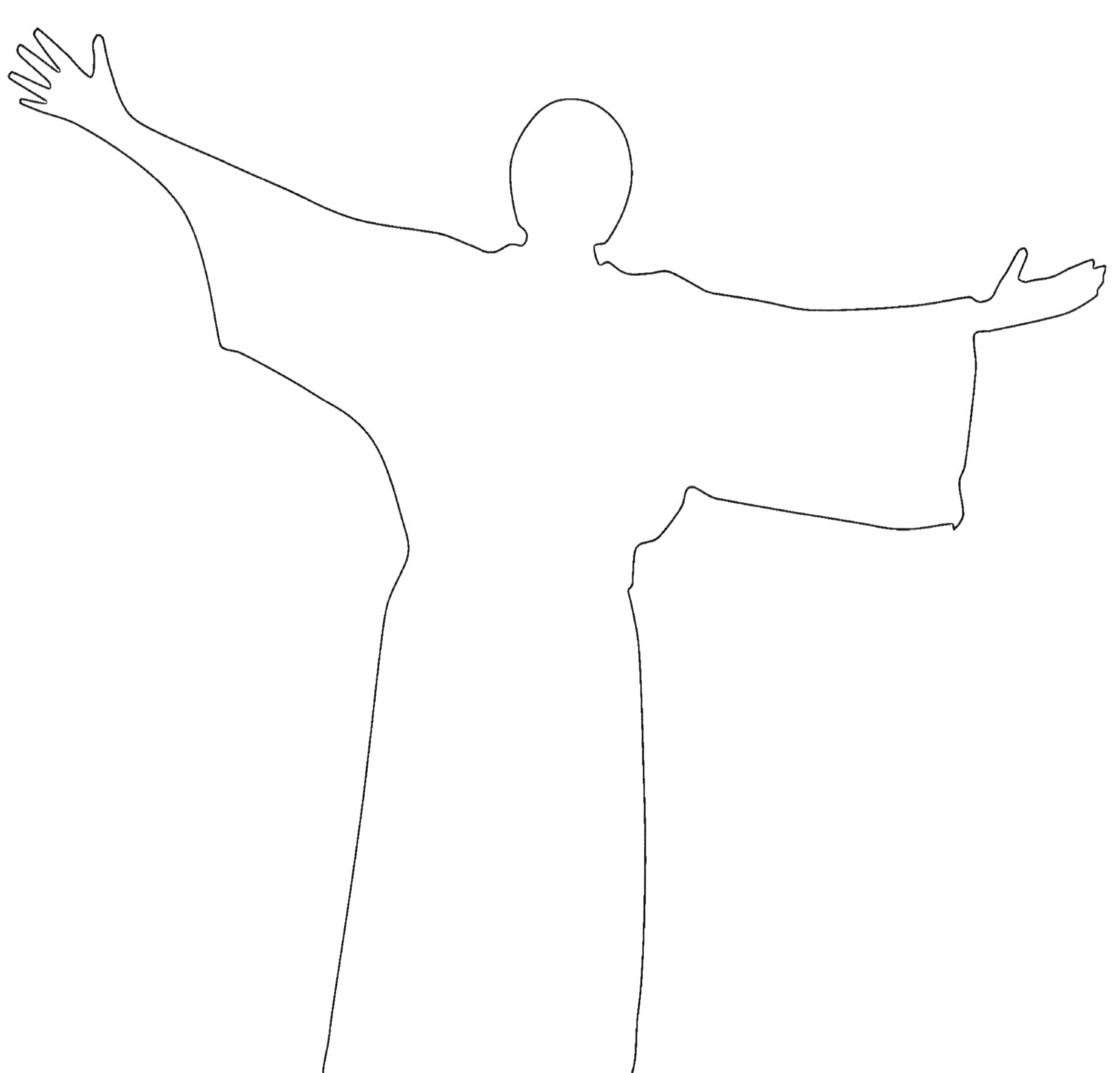

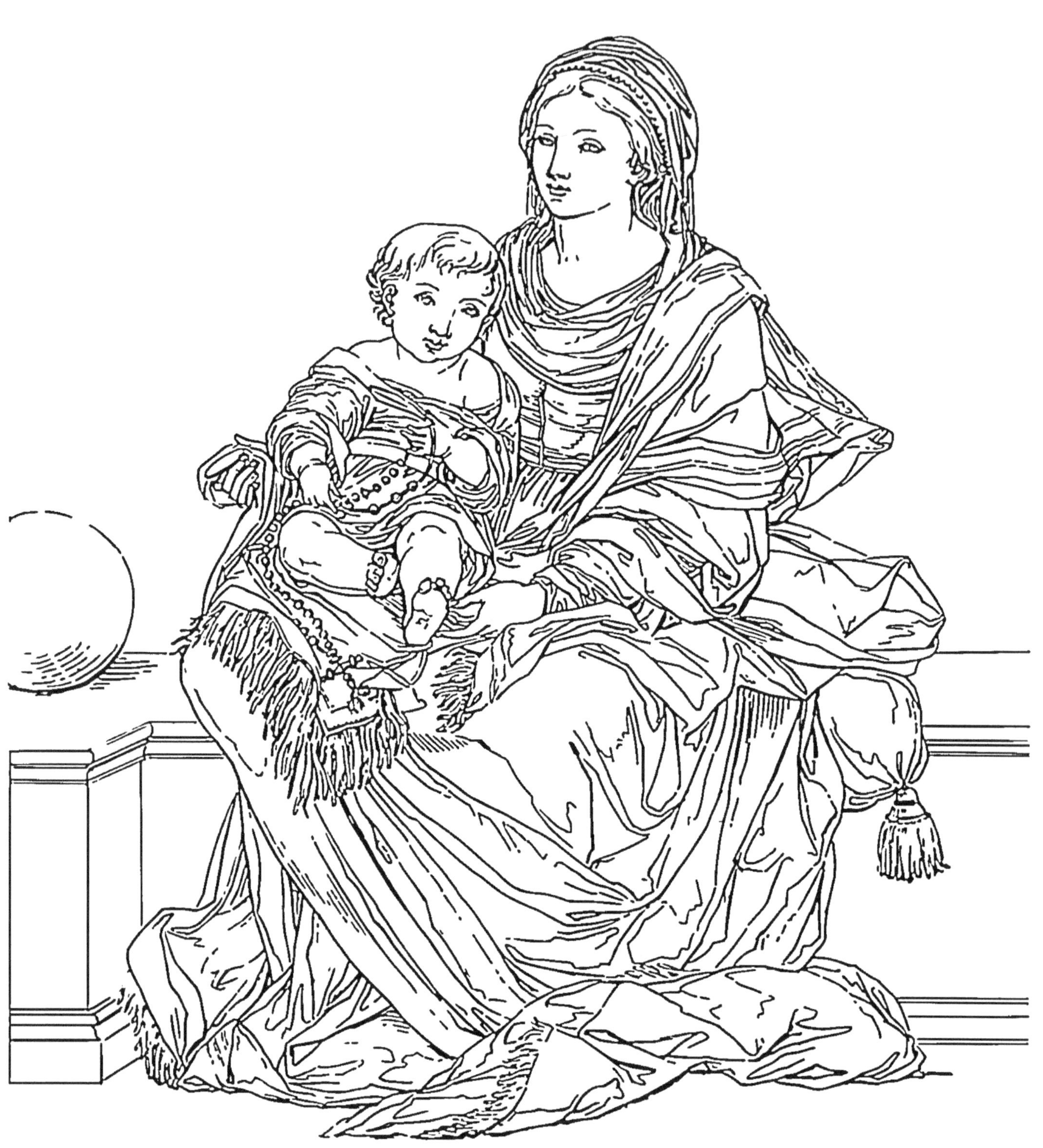

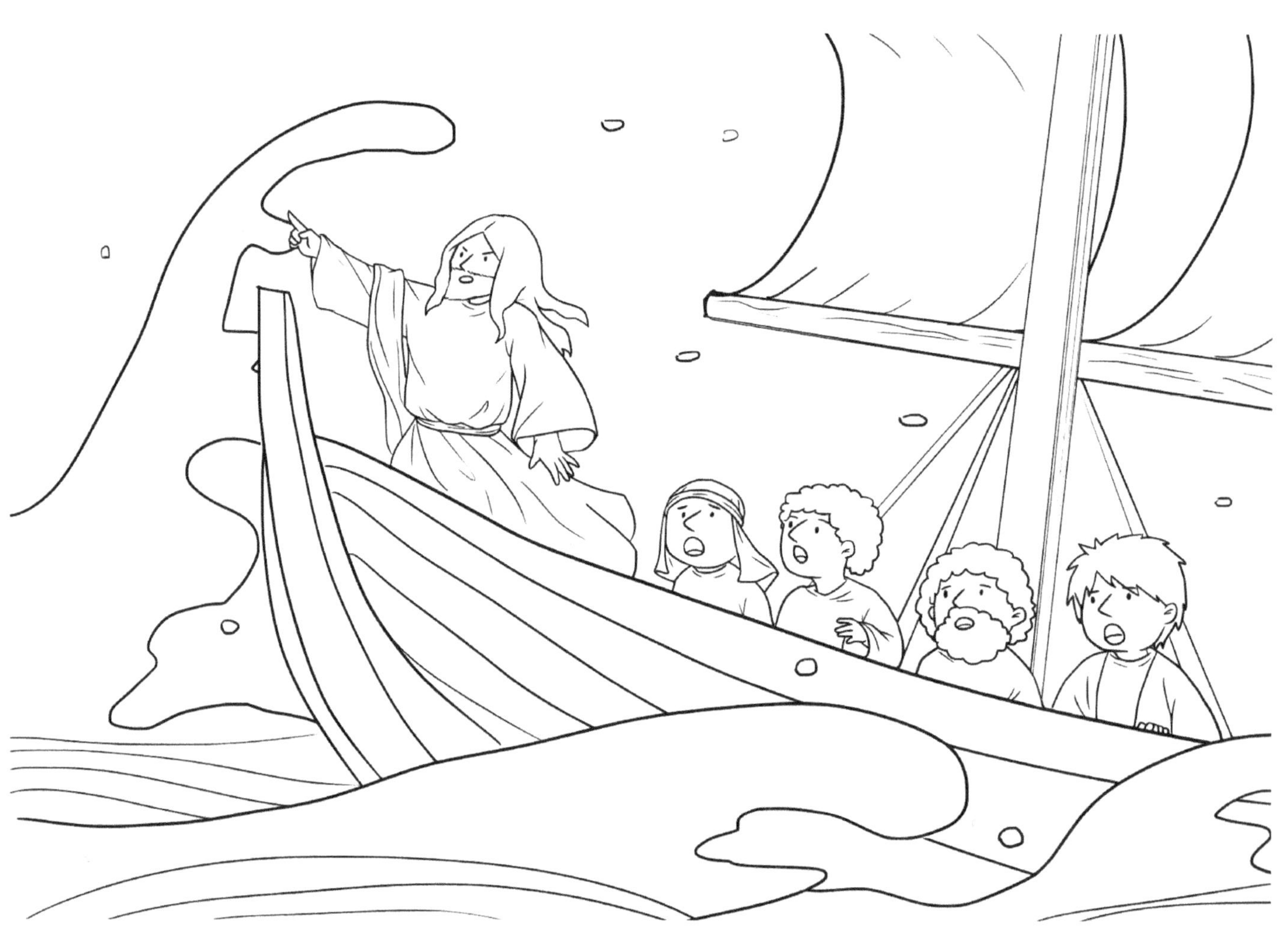

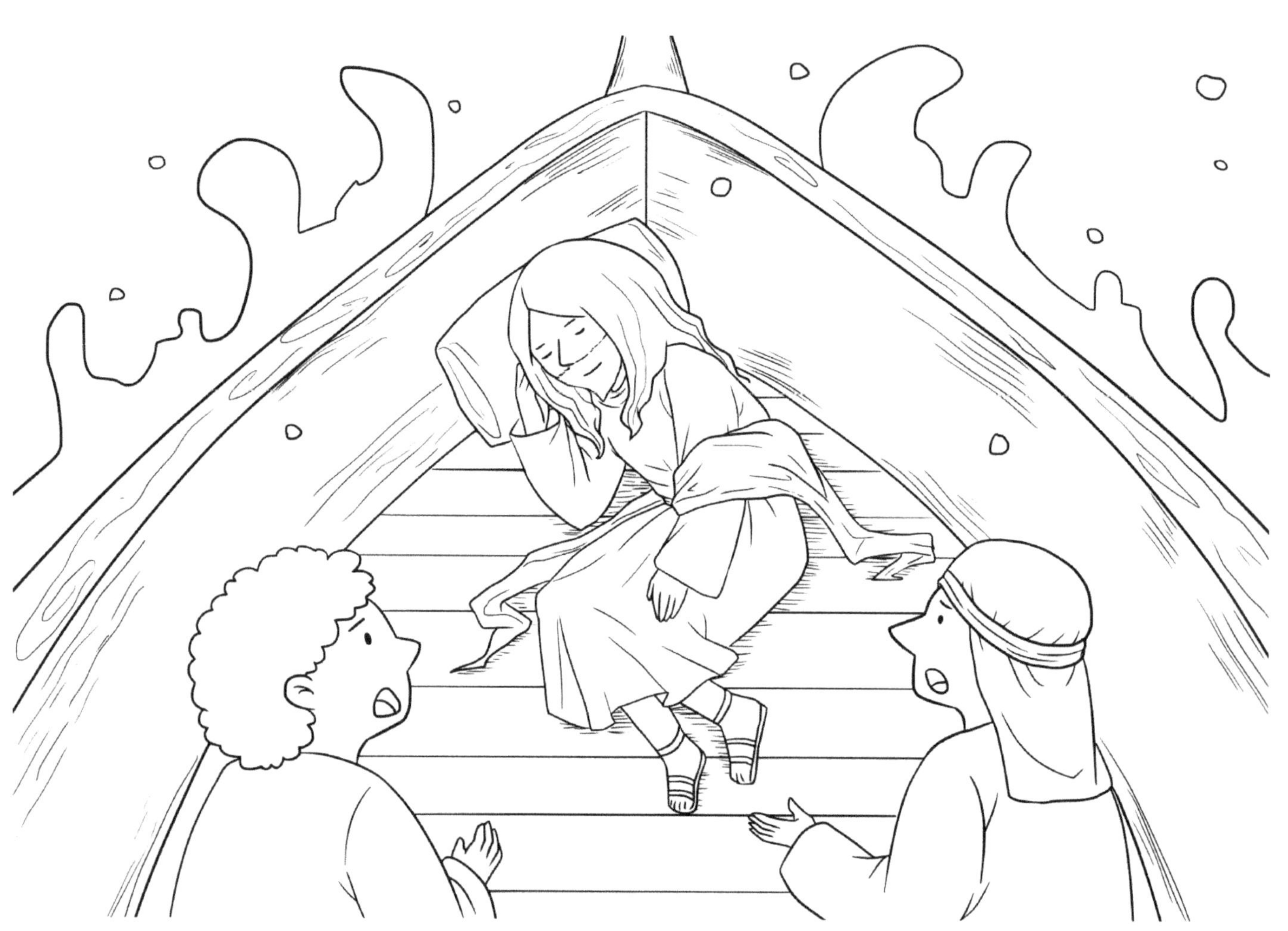

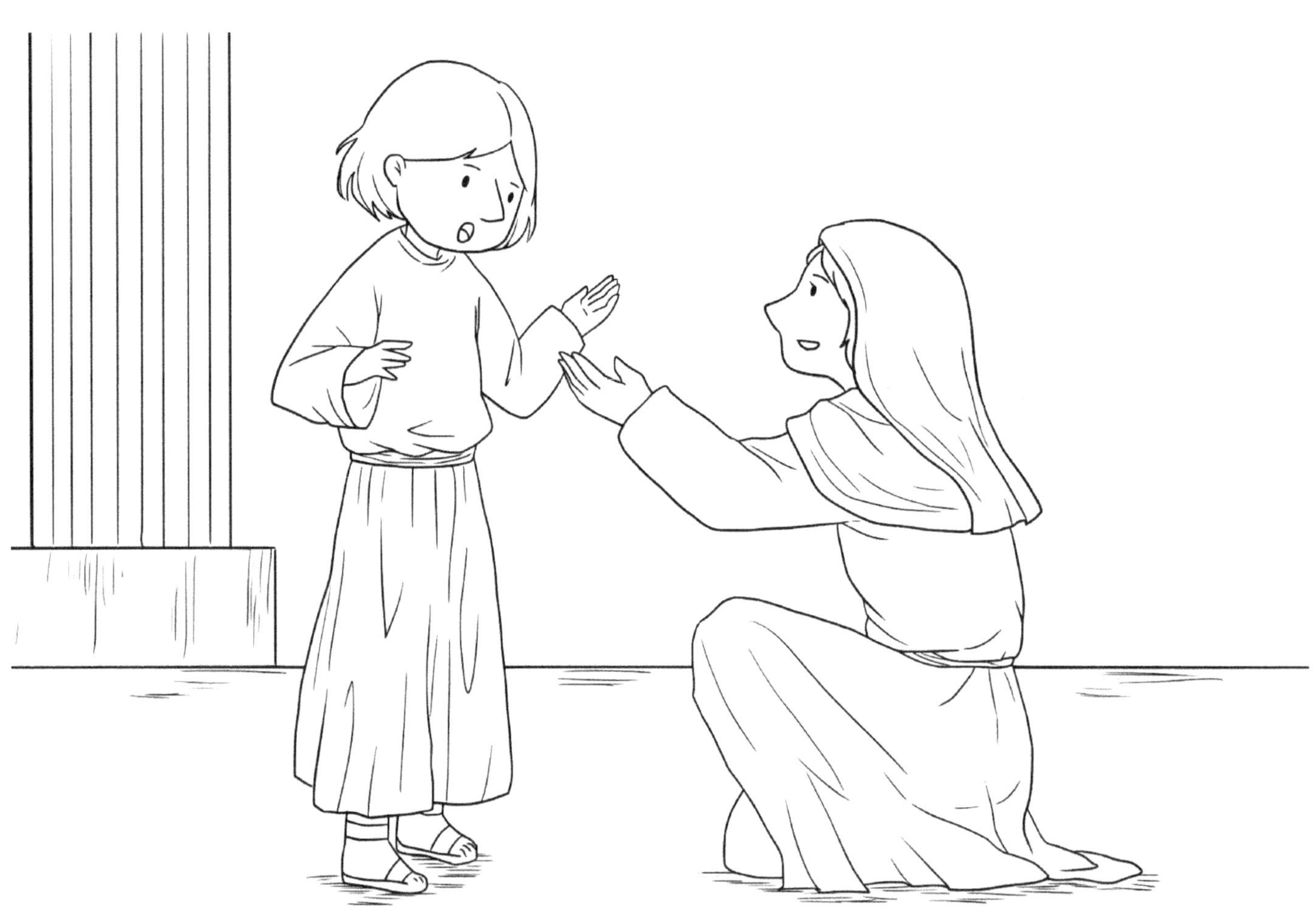

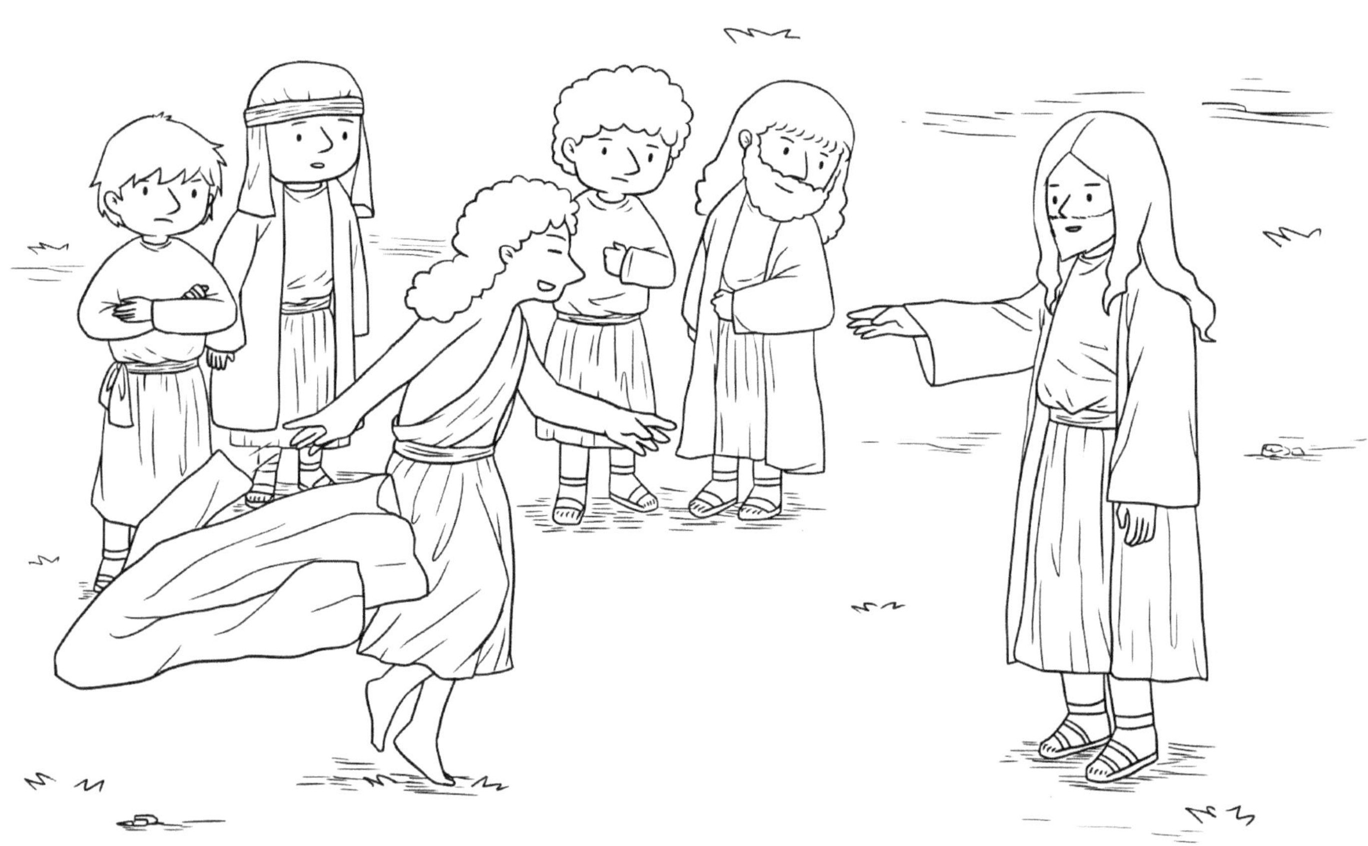

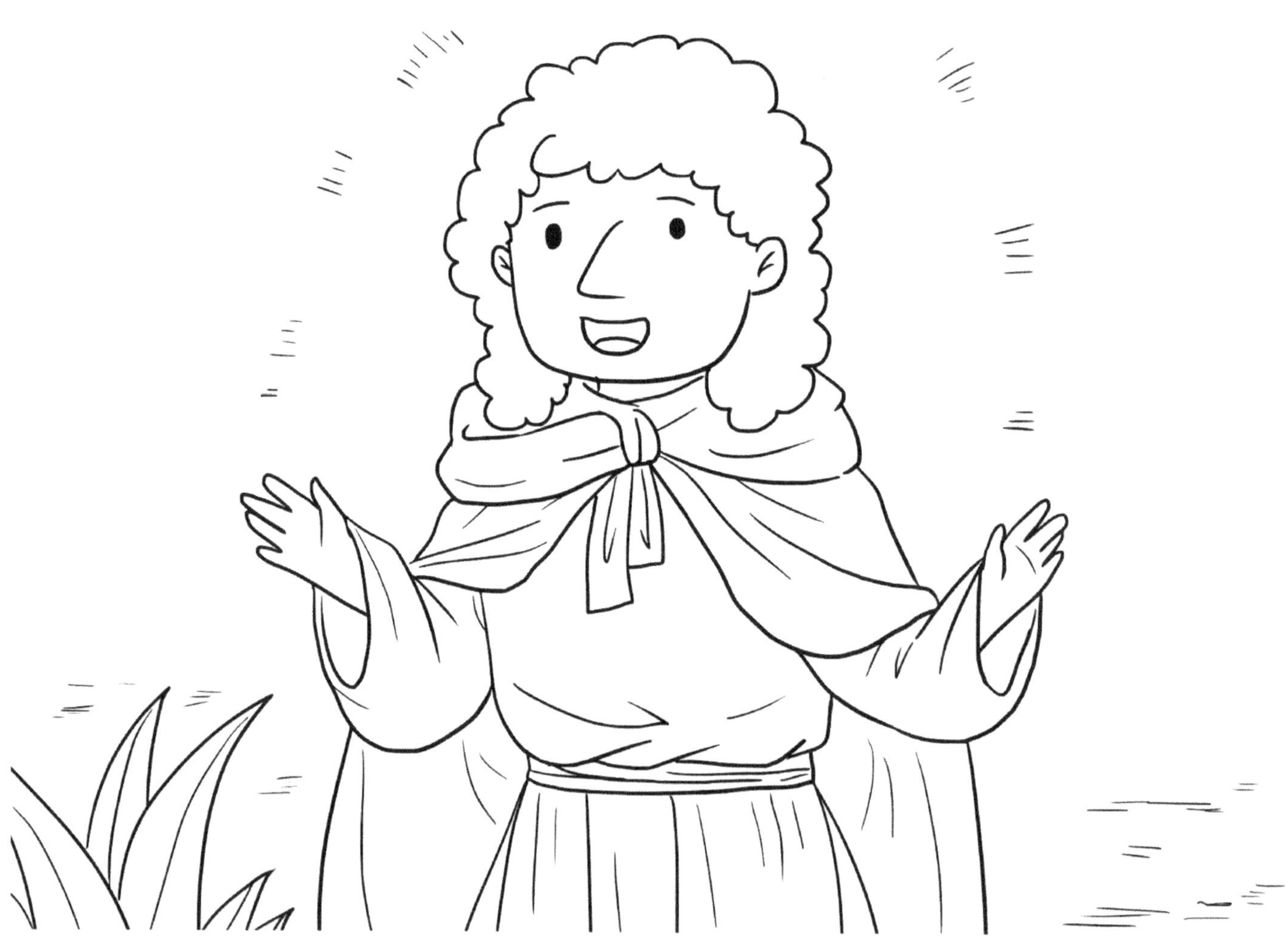

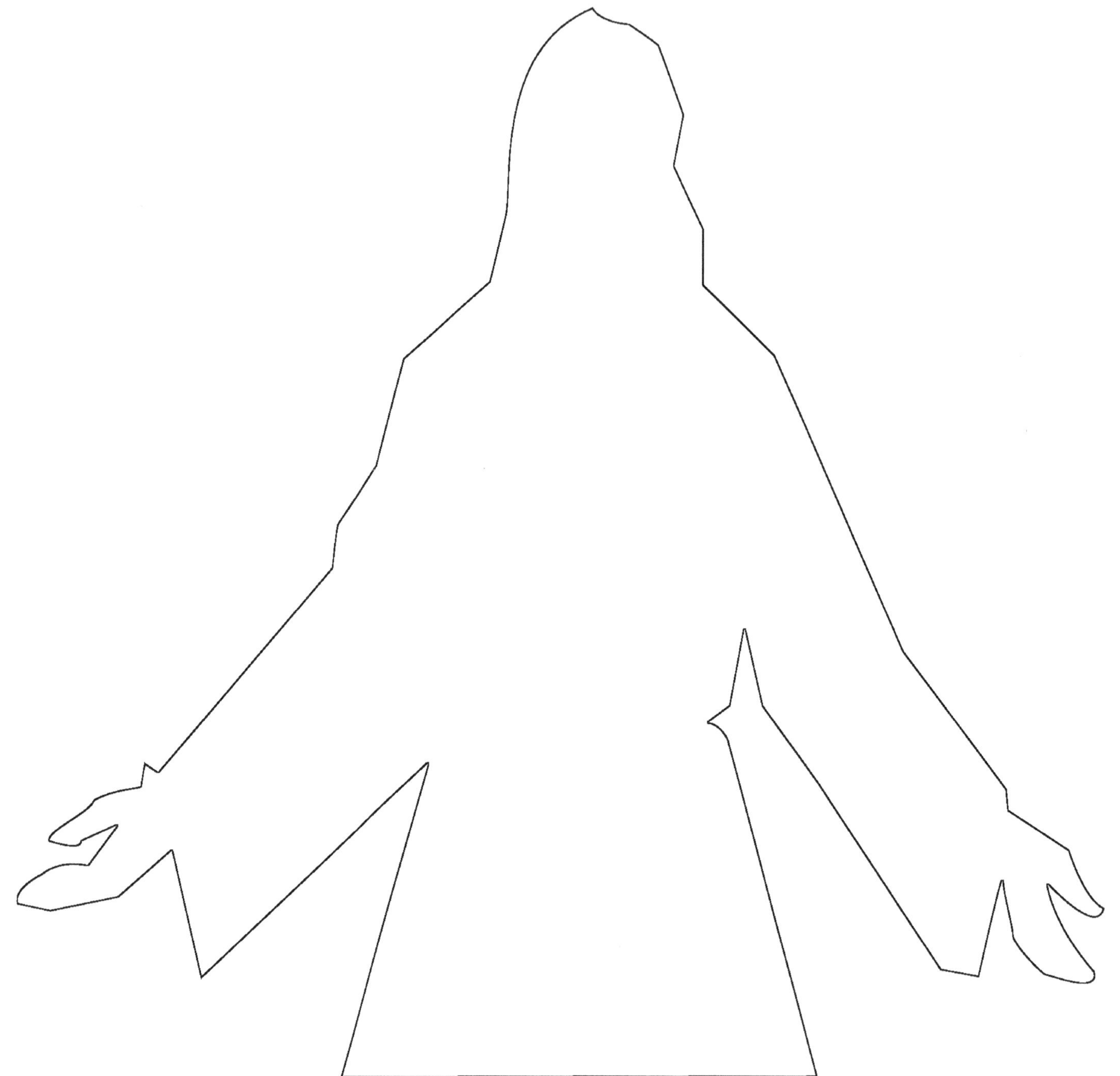

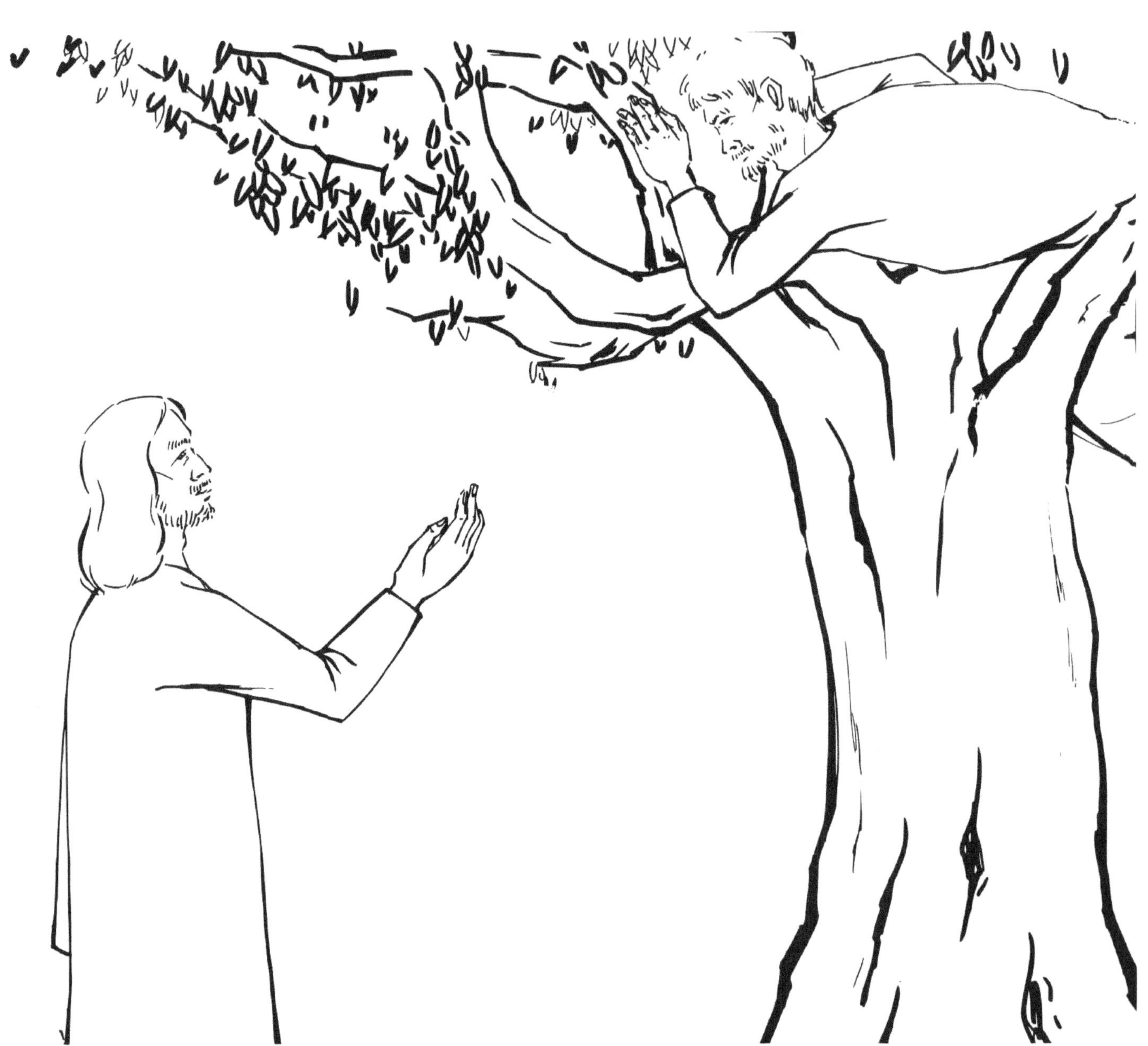

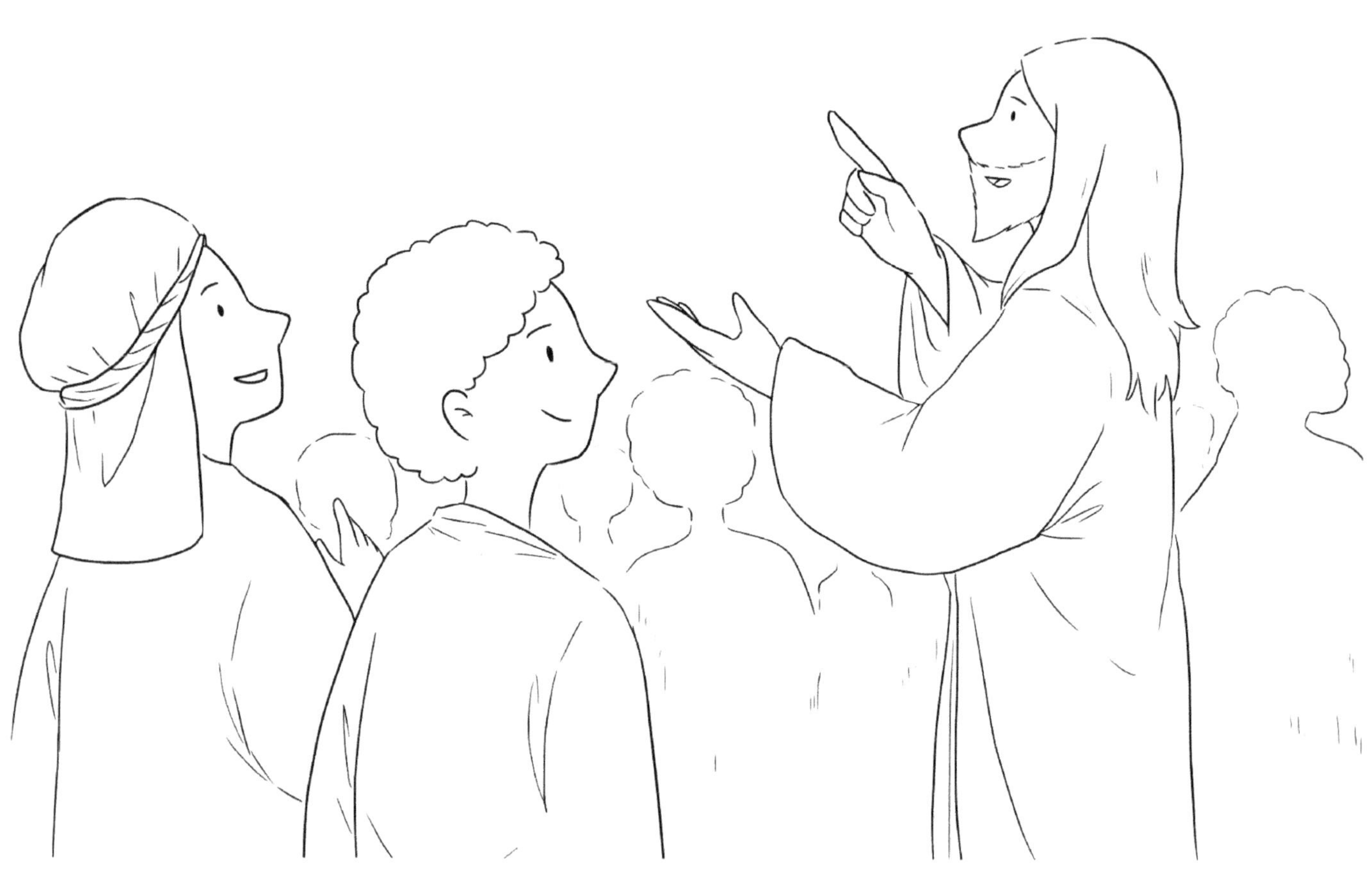

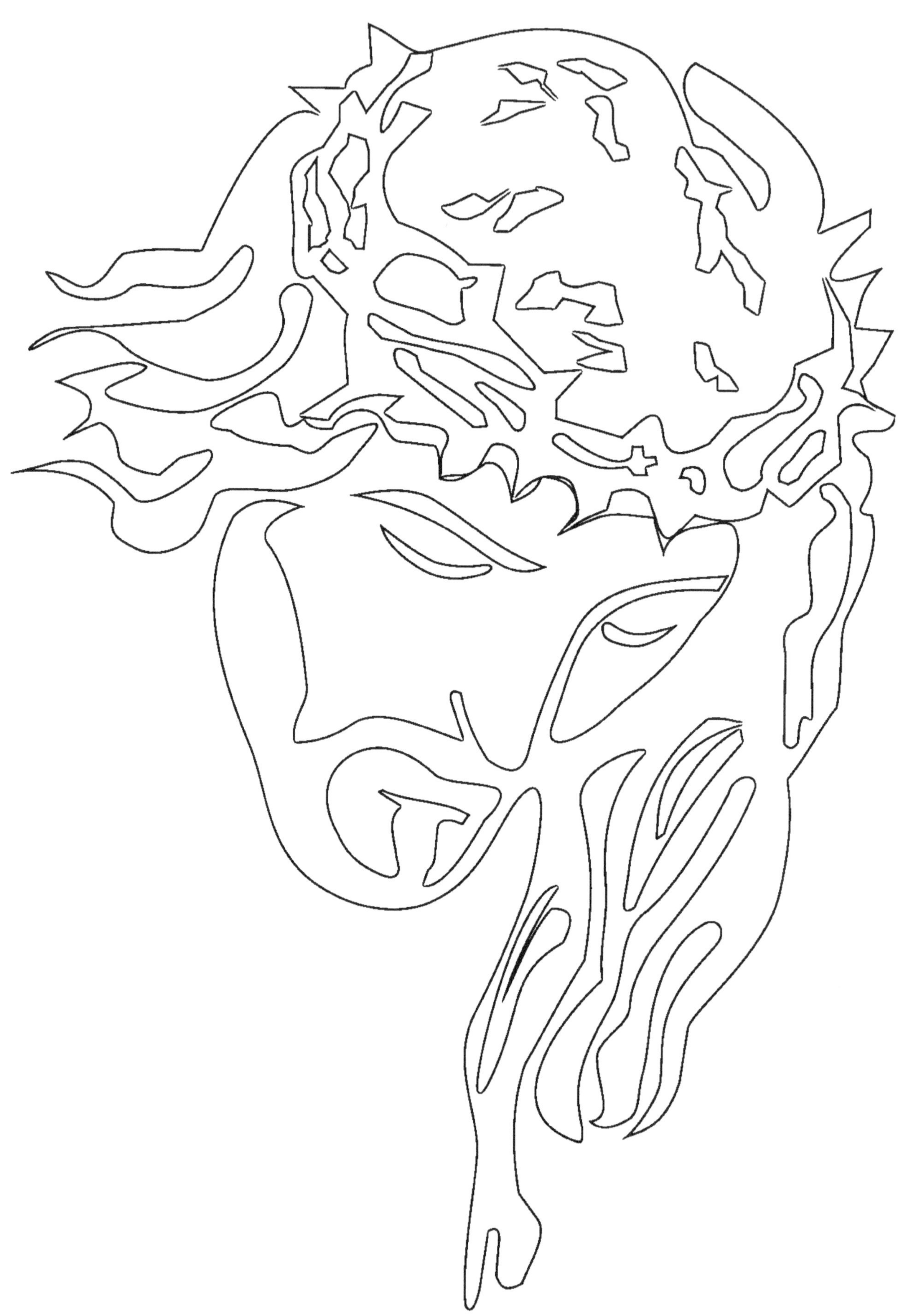

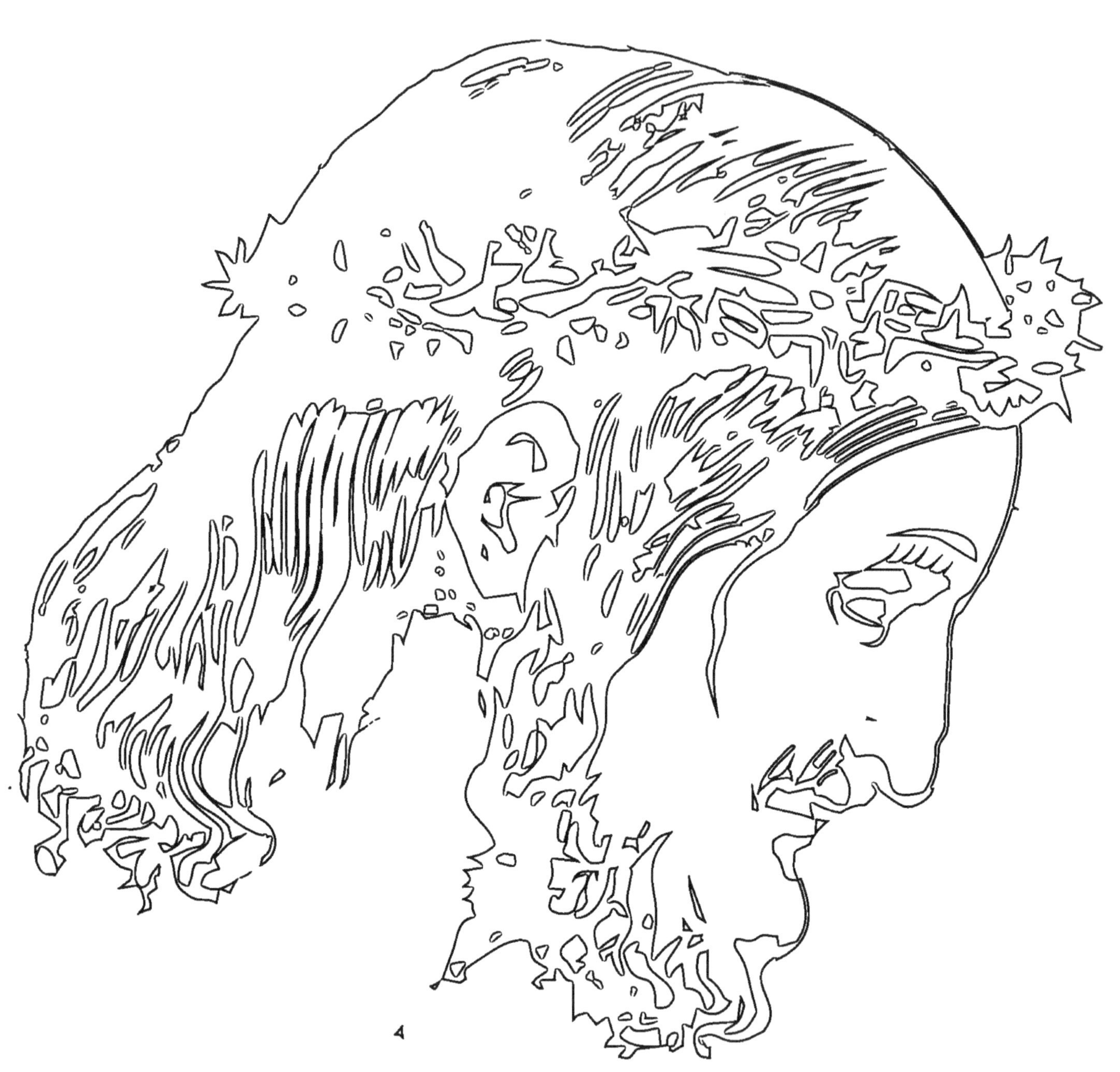

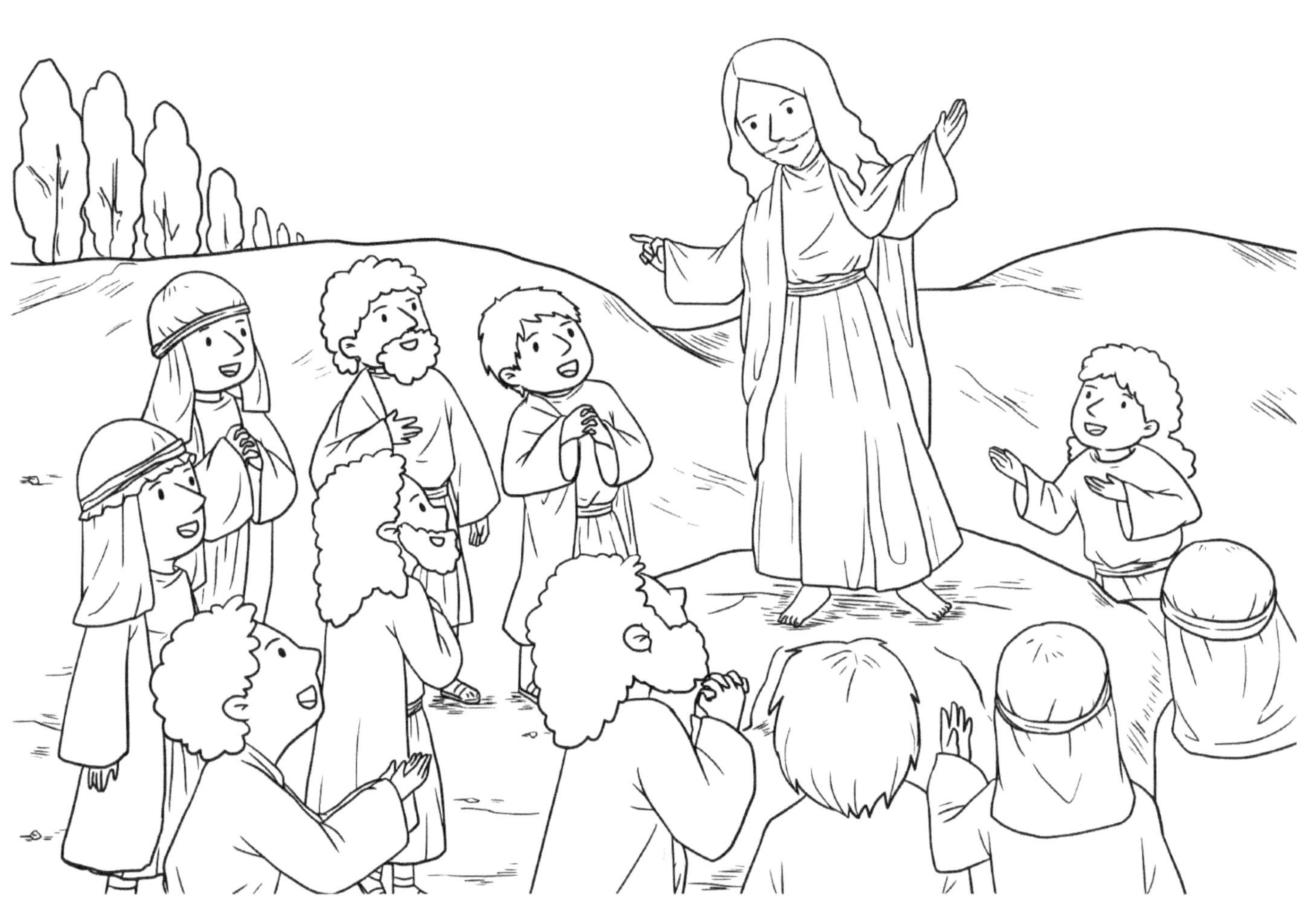

KyrillosCaesar

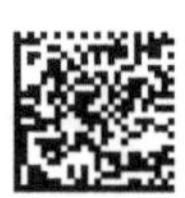

www.ingramcontent.com/pod-product-compliance
Lightning Source LLC
Chambersburg PA
CBHW081811250726
48653CB00010B/3891